SIGNALS

Senior Authors
Carl B. Smith
Virginia A. Arnold

Linguistics Consultant
Ronald Wardhaugh

Macmillan Publishing Co., Inc.
New York

Collier Macmillan Publishers
London

This work is also published together with other works in a single volume under the title: *Echoes of Time,* copyright © 1983 Macmillan Publishing Co., Inc. Parts of this work were published in earlier editions of SERIES r.

Macmillan Publishing Co., Inc.
866 Third Avenue, New York, New York 10022
Collier Macmillan Canada, Inc.

Printed in the United States of America
ISBN 0-02-132150-7
9 8 7 6 5 4 3 2

ACKNOWLEDGMENTS

The publisher gratefully acknowledges permission to reprint the following copyrighted material:

"The Animal's Point of View," from *The Language of Animals* by Millicent E. Selsam. Copyright © 1962 by Millicent E. Selsam. By permission of William Morrow & Company.

"Commercials and You," by Dawn Kurth is reprinted with her permission.

"Daniel Craig," adapted from *Heroes of Journalism* by Elizabeth D. Squire. Copyright © 1974, Fleet Press Corporation, New York. By permission of the publisher.

"King Midas and the Golden Touch," adapted from the CBS Radio "Let's Pretend" script. By permission of CBS Radio.

"We Could Be Friends," from *The Way Things Are and Other Poems* by Myra Cohn Livingston (A Margaret K. McElderry Book). Copyright © 1974 by Myra Cohn Livingston. By permission of Atheneum Publishers and Marian Reiner for the author.

"What Do You Know About Newspapers?" is a group of newspaper articles. "Circus Comes to Town" by Nancy Weldon is reprinted and adapted from the *The Times-Picayune,* New Orleans, La. "Town Meetings" is included courtesy of *The Boston Globe.* "How Sweet It Is!" and "Solo to North Pole" are included with the permission of *The Associated Press.* "Skateboards Get Winterized" is included by permission of *The Christian Science Monitor.* Copyright © 1977 The Christian Science Publishing Society. All rights reserved. "Doggy Alibi Flops" is included by permission of *United Press International.* "Metrics Move Ahead" is adapted from an article by Ed Meagher. Copyright © 1978 *The Los Angeles Times.* Reprinted by permission.

"Write It Down!" adapted from *The First Book of Words* by Sam and Beryl Epstein. Copyright © 1954. Used by permission of Franklin Watts, Inc.

Illustrations: Ray Cruz, pp. 4-7; Ed Renfro, pp. 16-19; Jan Pyk, pp. 26, 27-33; Robert Van Nutt, pp. 34-39; Sal Murdocca, pp. 45-63; Uldis Klavins, pp. 76-88; Jan Pyk, p. 89. **Photographs:** Fran Allen © *Animals, Animals,* p. 10; Paul N. Bozek, pp. 11, 15 L; Jane Latta, pp. 11 R, 14; Robert Weinreb © 1975/*Bruce Coleman, Inc.,* p. 12; Russ Kinne © 1974/*Photo Researchers, Inc.,* p. 13; Hans Reinhard/*Bruce Coleman, Inc.,* p. 15 L; © Douglas Mazonowicz/*Monkmeyer Press Photo Service,* pp. 20, 21; UNESCO Photos, p. 22; © Prof. Frank Moore Cross, Jr., p. 23; *American School of Classical Studies at Athens,* p. 24 L; *The Bettmann Archive,* p. 24 R; *Wide World Photo,* p. 28; NASA, p. 29; Edith Reichman/*Monkmeyer Press Photo Service,* p. 30; Joe Cordo, pp. 42-43; Candace Cochrane, pp. 64-71; Eva Fuka, pp. 100-101.

4

Contents

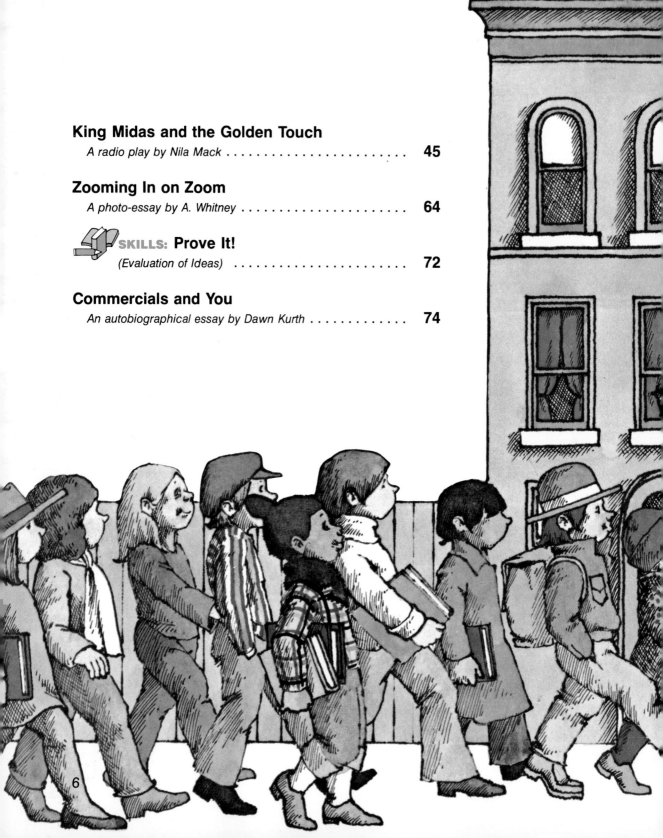

SIGNALS

From the time we are born, we are concerned with communication. Even before we can talk, our facial expressions, sounds, and gestures convey our feelings and thoughts to others. From the time animals are born, they also communicate. Animals send messages to each other using touch, smell, sight, and hearing. But communication among people is special. Only human beings have the ability to use words to convey messages.

By reading "Signals," you will find answers to the following questions: How do animals "talk" to each other without using words? How did people begin to write? How is a television show put together? What kinds of communication can be misleading? What new methods of communication might there be in the future?

As you read, think about how communication has developed and how it might change in the future. Think of all the ways you communicate with people and animals.

The Animal's Point of View

Millicent E. Selsam

Animals communicate with each other all the time. How do they do it? This essay presents some fascinating facts about the ways animals "talk" to each other.

Animals do not have a language like ours. They do not talk to each other in words and sentences. In fact, most animals cannot say a single word. But we only have to watch them to see that they communicate with each other by signals of some kind.

A school of minnows comes close to shore, and as we approach, their silvery bodies flash in unison. The whole school goes off together in another direction. Flocks of starlings come in to roost on a winter evening and shift and turn and dive together with the greatest precision. The monkeys in a zoo, the dogs on a street, the chickens in a barnyard, the minnows, the starlings, and most other animals have ways of communicating with one another.

But how can we find out about their secret worlds? How can we be sure of what an animal sees, hears, tastes, or smells? It is easy enough to imagine that their worlds are just like ours. We find it natural to think that they see what we see, hear what we hear, and smell the same odors we do. But if you think this way, you are bound to make mistakes.

Once, as a young teacher-in-training, I was asked to get down on the floor and sing to a turtle. My supervisor was sure that turtles loved music. I asked her if she thought they preferred classical or jazz. "Classical," she said. So I got as close as I could to the turtle and sang a theme from a Beethoven symphony. The turtle wagged its head back and forth, "almost in time to the music," my boss said. But somebody should have told us that it could not possibly hear anything, since a turtle is deaf.

A snake is deaf, too. But you can read stories and see pictures of snake charmers in Indian bazaars playing music to charm their deadly poisonous cobra snakes. If you watch such a performance, it looks as though the snake is listening and responding to the music. But a scientist became interested in this response and did some tests. He blindfolded the cobra. Then he beat on tin cans and blew bugles near the cobra. There was no reaction. When the blindfolds were removed, the experimenter waved his arms around. The cobra immediately raised its head and spread its hood. So we found out that snakes are charmed not by the sound of music, but by the movements the snake charmer makes while playing.

Imagine yourself sitting in a living room with a dog beside you, a bird in a cage, and a fish swimming in an aquarium. Each is in its own world. The dog can't see colors and in general can't see as well as we do. But it can smell the faintest odors and hear much higher sounds that we can. The bird has keen eyes but hardly any sense of smell. The fish is nearsighted in its watery world, but has taste organs in its skin that make it sensitive to chemicals or dissolved food in the water. If we want to find out how fish communicate with fish, or dogs with dogs, we must find out what their particular worlds are like. We must look at animals from the animal's point of view.

Animal communication is a relatively new branch of science. Much information has only recently been discovered. Some ideas we now think are true may change with further experimental work. But that is the very nature of all science —ever-changing and developing.

Afterword

Scientists continue to study animal communication through carefully planned experiments and observations. Scientists now know that animal communication by odor is the most common form of communication. A rabbit, for example, will rub its chin on twigs and stones in passing. This rubbing will leave an odor. Other rabbits then "read" the odor to learn what animals have used the path earlier.

Some ants give off a special alarm odor. This odor serves two purposes at once. It warns nearby ants of danger. At the same time, it attracts distant ants that will come to the rescue.

Touch is also used by animals to communicate. One kind of spider plucks the rim of its web in a special rhythm. This plucking communicates the spider's presence to another spider resting within the web.

Animals send messages by sight and sound, too. A fish may flick its tail or spread its fin. Other fish see and respond to this message. Many of the sounds of animal communication are familiar: dogs bark, birds chirp, lions growl. Other sounds too high for humans to hear are used by bats, moths, whales, and porpoises.

What might be learned in the future about animal communication? What kinds of nonverbal signals might people be sending out? Do animals respond to them? How? What can we learn about the world by "listening in" as animals communicate? These and other questions may someday be answered as scientists continue to study and experiment, observe and record, the communication of animals.

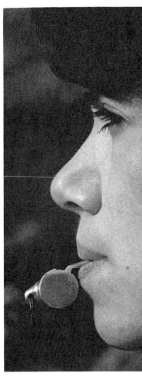

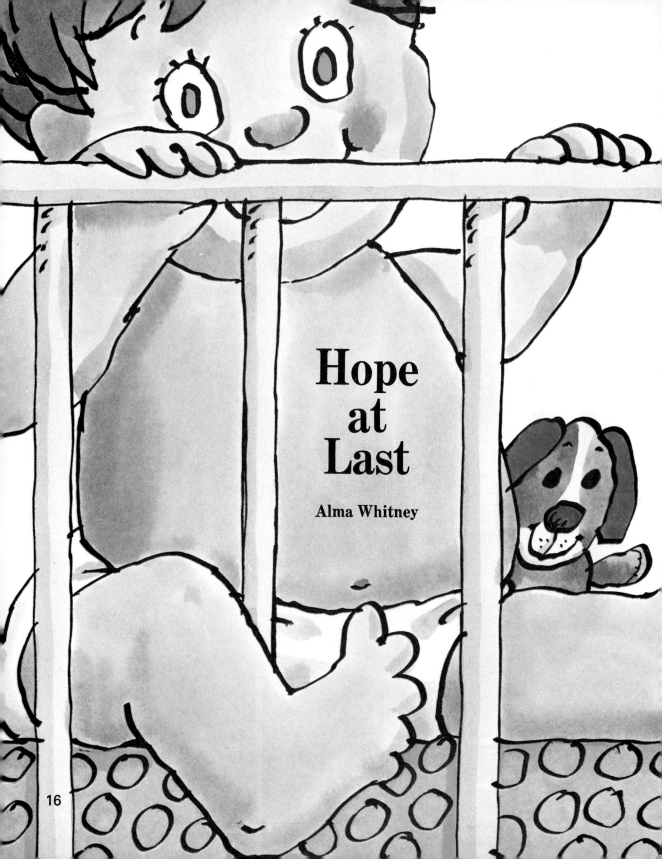

Hope
at
Last

Alma Whitney

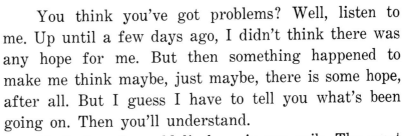

You think you've got problems? Well, listen to me. Up until a few days ago, I didn't think there was any hope for me. But then something happened to make me think maybe, just maybe, there is some hope, after all. But I guess I have to tell you what's been going on. Then you'll understand.

Each day, I would lie here in my crib. The most unbelievable things would happen. Grownups, large people, would keep walking by and looking down at me.

"A boo-boo-boo," would say the one with the blond hair. She's my mother.

"Wutch-um, wutch-um, wutch-um," the one with the whiskers would say. He's my father.

And every so often, the top of a smaller person's head would go by. That would be my big brother, Fred. He wouldn't say much at all. Just "ugh" and "ick," sometimes.

I was really getting worried. "How will I ever learn to talk right at this rate?" I kept thinking. I knew people didn't talk to each other the way they talked to me. For example, my mother would say, "Walter, is it time for the news on television yet?"

And my father would answer, "In a few minutes, Agnes."

Not one "a-boo" or "wutch-um" that time.

And of course, the people on the television didn't say "hozum babee." They'd say really terrific things like "traffic report" and "this evening's presentation."

Just the other day I was having my lunch. According to my mother, the menu was eggsies and pearsies. But when Fred asked my mother if he could have eggsies and pearsies, my mother said, "Don't talk like that, Fred. That's baby talk."

In my whole life, which happens to be about six months, I have never said anything like "eggsies" or "pearsies." As a matter of fact, I have never said much at all. That is, until a few days ago. But I must say that, when I did finally speak, what I said made quite a commotion.

I was lying on my back. I was looking up at my bird mobile when my mother decided to peek down at me. Now I usually make a lot of different sounds. But that day I said "ah-ah" right to my mother's face.

"Walter," my mother called. "Walter, come here. The baby just said 'mama.'"

My father came running into the room. He looked down at me. Since it seemed to make everybody so excited, I said it again. "Ah-ah."

"Nonsense," my father said. "The baby just said 'dada.'"

MAMA DADA WATER DOG SPAGHETTI

"Mama," said my mother looking down at me.

"Ah-ah-ah-ah," I answered.

"Da-da-da-da," said my father.

"Ah-ah-ah-ah," I said again.

Since then, I've said "ah-ah" quite a bit. My mother has decided that it also means "water" and "dog." At least, I think she has. Every time she brings me a bottle of water, she says "whaaah-terrr." And when she gives me my little pink dog, she says "dahg." I say "ah-ah" to these things. And does she get excited!

Frankly, I think my father still believes I'm saying "dada." He keeps sneaking by my crib and whispering "dada." When I answer "ah-ah," he grins and says "a very intelligent baby!"

So you see, there seems to be some hope for me now. I haven't gotten it quite right yet. But I'm working on "ab-ab-ab" and "boo." I can't wait to hear what they think I'm saying then.

What I'm really looking forward to is the day when I can say fantastic words like "spaghetti" and "chocolate syrup." You've got to admit, they're pretty terrific. But for now I would really settle for "Please ma, don't make me eat that squash again." I hate spitting the stuff out and crying. But that seems to be the only way I can make myself understood.

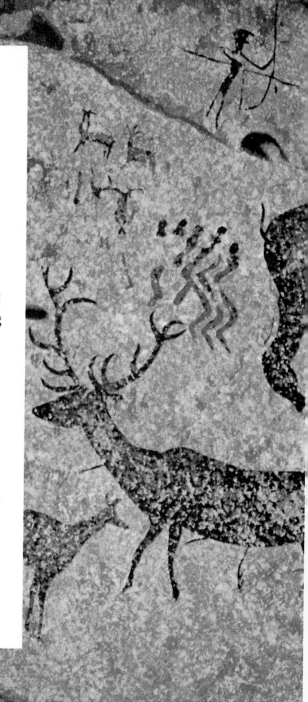

WRITE IT DOWN!

Sam and Beryl Epstein

The invention of writing happened very slowly, and it took place so long ago that no one really knows much about it. You can guess why it happened, though.

People could speak their thoughts. They knew how to put their thoughts into the sounds we call words. But they didn't know how to keep the thoughts.

You know that if you tell somebody something, the person may forget it. If you put your thought into written words, however, the person can look at the words again and again. Whenever the person looks at the words they will say the same thing.

When your words are written down they can't be forgotten.

All writing is just a way of keeping thoughts. Newspapers and magazines and books are thoughts written down so that people can read them, whenever they want to, so that they can keep the thoughts forever and even hand them down to their children's children.

The first kind of writing was what is called picture-writing. Today in America if we want to write about a dog, we write *DOG*. People who did picture-writing made a picture of a dog, instead, like this:

After a time, people found that they couldn't always make a picture that looked like the thing that was in their minds. They could make a picture that looked like a dog, but they couldn't make a picture that looked like "good" or "comfort" or "true." If people wanted to put down thoughts such as "good" or "comfort" or "true," they had to think of special pictures that would express those ideas. When people make pictures that express ideas, they are said to be writing *ideographs*. *Graph* is from an ancient Greek word that means "writing." You can see that *ideograph* means "idea-writing."

Left: Cave painting found in Bicorp, Spain

Right: Cave painting found in Caballos, Spain

The Chinese still use ideographs when they write today. Some of the ideographs are so simple that they are almost picture-writing. When the Chinese want to talk about a tree, for example, they say the word *mu*, which means tree or wood in Chinese. But when they want to write about a tree they don't write the letters *m* and *u*. Instead they draw a little picture of a tree, like this: 木 . If they want to write about trees, they don't add a letter *s* to their word, as English-speaking people do. They make a picture of two trees, like this: 木木. The picture of the two trees means "more than one tree," or "forest."

Probably when people first used picture-writing they made whatever kind of pictures they wanted to make. After a while, all the people in one part of the world agreed that certain pictures would mean certain things. Then they could understand each other's writing.

In the ancient land of Phoenicia, about three thousand years ago, people who wanted to write down the idea of an ox made this little picture: ⌣ , which looked to them like the horns of an ox. If they wanted to write "door," they made this picture: ⌢ . Their word for ox

Text and drawing on manuscript page by Chinese author/artist Tsen Yen-Tung

was *aleph*. Their word for door was *daleth*.

The Phoenicians had to learn a new picture for every single word. It took a long time to learn the pictures for all the words. So, after a while, the Phoenicians began to work out a new method of writing. Instead of using the picture ⌣ to mean *aleph*, they used that picture for the first sound in the word *aleph*—the sound of A. Instead of using ⌢ to mean door, or *daleth,* they used it for the first sound in the word *daleth,* the sound of D. If the Phoenicians had wanted to write the English word *AD*, they would have written it like this: ⌣ ⌢

The Phoenicians were the only people in the world ever to develop a true alphabet—a system of signs to represent sounds.

After a time the Greeks borrowed most of the signs the Phoenicians were using. They changed some of them to suit themselves. They turned the sign for A, ⌣, upside down, for example, and made it like this: ⌢ . They also added a few new signs of their own, because the Greek language had some sounds in it that the Phoenician language didn't have.

Phoenician writing on The Nora Stone found in Nora, Sardinia

Then the Romans began to use many of the signs the Greeks were using, and they changed the signs too. Finally the signs the Romans used, plus a few others, were used for the writing of English words. The old Phoenician sign for ox had become the letter *A*, and the old sign for a door had become the letter *D*. The other letters of the Roman alphabet developed in the same way from those long-ago signs first used in picture-writing.

Greek writing on stone tablet from 480 B.C.

Roman coin

The Phoenician word for	The Phoenician sign was	Greeks changed this to	Romans changed this to	
ox was aleph	∢ or ∀	ᗡ then to A	A	A
house was beth	ᕫ or ᒫ	ᗷ then to B	B	B
camel was gimel	∧ or ∧	⌐ then to ⌐	C	C
door was daleth	◿ or △	△	D	D
window was he	⩾	⪡ then to E	E	E
hook was vau	Y or ⋔	⋀ then lost	F	F
		⌐ then to ⌐	G	G
fence was cheth	⊟ or ᛗ	⊟ then to H	H	H
hand was yod	Z	⋛ then to I	I	I
				J
palm was kaph	Y or ⋊	⋊ then to k	K	K
rod was lamed	L or ᒪ	⌐ then to ∧	L	L
water was mem	⧓ or ⋈	M then to M	M	M
fish was nun	⋎ or ⋺	⋎ then to N	N	N
eye was ayin	○	○	O	O
mouth was pe	⅃ or ⅁	⅂ then to ⊓	P	P
knot was koph	Φ	Ϙ then lost	Q	Q
head was resh	◁ or ⋪	⋟ then to P	R	R
tooth was shin	W or ⋃	Σ	S	S
mark was tahv	T or X	T	T	T
		V then to V		U
			V	V
				W
support was samekh	⯠ or ᛝ	⯠ then to ☰	X	X
			Y	Y
weapon was zayin	⊥ or ⋋	I then to Z	Z	Z

Say It With Symbols

The idea of a world-wide system of communication based on symbols rather than words has interested people for many years. One such system has been developed by a man named C.K. Bliss. This system is called *Semantography*, which means "writing for meaning." Most of the symbols are drawn to look like the things they name. So it is easy to remember what the symbols mean. Here are some examples:

↑   λ   △   ✗

tree   **man**   **woman**   **bird**

Of course, you need to be able to show actions as well as the names of things. In Semantography, actions are shown by placing a ∧ above a symbol. Here are two examples:

⊙   is the symbol for eye

⊙̂   is the symbol for seeing

∧   is the symbol for legs and feet

∧̂   is the symbol for walking

In Semantography, symbols are combined to mean different things. Here are some examples:

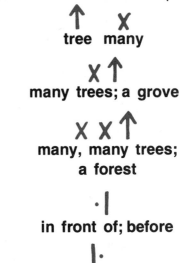

↑   ✗
tree   **many**

✗ ↑
many trees; a grove

✗ ✗ ↑
many, many trees; a forest

·|
in front of; before

|·
behind; after

Here is a sentence written in Semantography. Can you read it?

λ   +   △   λ̂   ·| ↑

Now try writing this sentence in Semantography: *The man sees a bird behind the tree.*

Would you like to create your own system of symbols? If so, remember to keep your symbols simple. Use as few symbols as possible, and keep your system easy to read.

What Do You Know About
NEWSPAPERS?

Any time you want to find out what's happening around the world or around the block, turn to a newspaper. You couldn't have done that in America in 1690 because there was only one newspaper, and it ran for only one issue. But in our world today, it's easy to turn to a newspaper. More than 62½ million papers are sold every day in the United States alone. It's hard to imagine life without a newspaper.

Glance at the front page of a newspaper. The first thing you are sure to notice is the paper's name, or *logo*. As you start reading, you will find many *headlines,* the attention-getting titles of news articles.

If you want to know who wrote a story, you can sometimes find the writer's name in a *byline*. To learn more about a photograph, just read the description, or *caption,* under it.

You might be confused when an article seems to be cut off in the middle of a sentence. Don't worry! You'll see the *jumpline*. What is a jumpline? It's a note telling you where to find the conclusion of the story.

To take a close look at the form of a newspaper, just turn the page . . .

Morning Edition

The Daily Banner

Weather: Sunny and clear.

20 cents   **Saturday, June 1, 1985**   *Vol. CCCXL*

A LONG WAY FROM HOME: Explorer reaches North Pole.

How Sweet It Is

Madison, Wis. (AP) — The honeybee buzzed in yesterday as Wisconsin's state insect. In a ceremony, the governor approved a bill to make the honeybee the state insect. Honeybees in the state last year made more than 10.2 million pounds of honey. This gave the state fifth-place honors in honey production.

Solo to the North Pole

Tokyo (AP) — A Japanese explorer became the first person to reach the North Pole alone by dog sled. The 500-mile trip took 57 days.

First word of the deed was sent to the Smithsonian Institution in Washington, D.C. It was sent through an automatic device the explorer was carrying. This device sent a beam to Washington by way of a satellite.

Two photographers were flown to the North Pole to take the explorer's picture. At the same time, the photographers also picked up the diary he had been keeping. He is expected to stay in the North Pole area for several days. He started his trip from the Canadian Arctic.

U.S. plans another space flight to ringed planet, Saturn.

Space Flight

It has been announced that the United States is planning another space flight to explore Saturn, the sixth planet from the sun.

Saturn has long been of interest because it is surrounded by rings. With every flight, scientists hope to discover more about Saturn's hundreds of rings.

No further information on the nature of the flight has been made public.

Metrics Move Ahead

From Inches to Centimeters

By Ed Meagher

The United States is moving closer to the metric age. Many grade school youngsters are studying metric measurements for the first time.

Some experimental classes in metrics have already been held. Entire schools have also been introducing metrics on their own. Nationwide, more and more people are beginning to learn and use metrics.

Some teachers still do not feel that the schools or the nation is ready for metrics teaching. They say that textbooks are not in agreement on how metrics should be taught. They also feel that some schools will teach metrics, but others may not.

But the change to metrics is surely happening. The nation decided to change when the Metrics Conversion Act was passed in

(Continued on Next Page)

Metrics Move Ahead
(Continued from Previous Page)

1975. As a result, Americans in years to come will increasingly use meters, kilometers, grams, and so on. Good-by to pints, quarts, and ounces.

UNDER THE BIG TOP: Circus plans two-week stay.

Circus Comes to Town

By Nancy Weldon

With the words "Ladies and gentlemen and children of ALL ages . . ." the circus began on Thursday. Glittering and in some cases death-defying acts followed. They were led by a performer's breath-taking wire walk 200 feet above the floor.

The entire performance was full of thrills. One highlight was the trapeze act, which received plenty of applause and cheers. The biggest problem the crowd of thousands had was deciding which ring to watch.

During the second half of the show, the houselights were dimmed. Trainers put the big cats through their act. The "children of all ages" had a good time.

Statewide Baseball Scores

Columbus 4	Loomis 2
Wright 3	Eugene 0
Everett 5	Pacific 4
Louis 1	Randolph 0
Rockwell 5	Drummond 2

Sports Today

Blue Jays vs. Bears at Main High School, 6:00 P.M.

Summer Sports Program Announced

This week the mayor outlined the city's summer sports program. Training will be offered in tennis, jogging, swimming, and other activities.

The classes are free and open to the public. However, the mayor encouraged anyone interested to sign up for classes as soon as possible to avoid disappointment.

The program is to have a staff of five teachers. There are still two positions to be filled. Mayor Andersen said that anyone who has had sports training experience could apply at Town Hall.

The program will start in the middle of June and last until the end of August. So sports fans — pick up your rackets, start running, and dive in!

Skateboards Get Winterized

By Ross Atkin

In some northern countries, skateboarders can practice their sport year-round in indoor skateboard parks. But why go indoors when Old Man Winter arrives? Ask Swiss youngsters. They are changing their skateboards into skiboards. By replacing wheels with small runners, they turn their boards into mini-sleds. Then they can skiboard down snow-covered hills. The idea for skiboards may have come from skiers, who keep training during the summer by using skis on wheels.

The Daily Banner

Founded in 1851

Charles Brooks, *Publisher*

Metric: Yes or No?

The debate about whether America should go metric continues. The case for giving up inches and gallons for meters and liters is based on several ideas. The metric system is more efficient and practical. Also, it is now the way of the world. Only the United States and some small nations cling to the old measurements. Fully 90% of the world's population enjoys the ease of metrics. We have argued for years in favor of the metric system.

Letters

Editor:

What in the world is going on? I thought that we had changed to metrics in this country. But everywhere I look — even in this newspaper — I still see the old measurements. Don't send me this newspaper anymore!

Elizabeth Kendall Schlesinger

Editor:

I agree with your editorial of last Sunday on litter. Let's have the police give out more tickets to litterers. Maybe a $25 fine would help some people break their bad habits. Those of us who use public trash cans support you completely.

I. M. Tidy

Editor:

Increase police ticketing of litterers? Ridiculous! Our police have more important things to do. We can all help. When was the last time you picked up a piece of stray litter to deposit it in a trash can?

Lee Tucker

Editor:

We feel a traffic light is needed on the corner of Bergen and Sixth Avenue. Children have to cross that street to reach Bergen School. Traffic is heavy, and the cars and trucks travel rapidly. Let's put up a traffic light *before* a child is hurt.

S. Lopez
R. Smith

Editor:

I agree with your recent editorial on city parks. These parks belong to all of us. Everyone should help keep them clean. Who wants to picnic or stroll through a dirty park? Down with litter!

Anna Choy

Doggy Alibi Flops

Parkersburg, W. Va. (UPI) — A young man told the judge he could not have been going 45 mph in a 35 mph zone. A dog was chasing his car at the time. The driver argued that no dog could run that fast. He said the encyclopedia proved he was right. It says that the fastest dog, the greyhound, can only run 35 mph. The dog chasing his car was just a common breed. But Judge Anne McDonough found him guilty anyway. She fined him $40.

Town News

- Chatham — Last minute decisions were made to hire two more police officers and four more firefighters.
- Boylston — The Fire Department will get a new pumper. A new heating system will be installed in the town library.
- Weymouth — The Fore River will be dredged. The vote for this project was 100 votes for and 38 against.
- Spring Valley — Everyone is invited to the annual pancake breakfast on Saturday. Doors open at 8:00 A.M. and close when the batter is gone.

Classified Advertisements

HELP WANTED: Babysitter. Weekdays. $1.50 an hour. Call Mr. Drake. 366-1128.

HELP WANTED: Stock person. Williams Department Store. Experienced only. 722-8815.

HELP WANTED: Someone to care for yard while owner is on vacation. 776-4242.

HELP WANTED: Salesperson. Kim's Flower Shop. Apply in person. 310 South Main St.

FOR RENT: One bedroom apartment. Call 788-3040.

FOR SALE: Drums. Like new. Best offer. 388-4910.

FOR SALE: Piano. Just tuned. Best offer. Call 905-2336.

FOR SALE: Used boy's bike. Blue. $40. Call 331-9801.

LOST: Black dog. Answers to Daisy. Reward. Call 744-5627.

FREE: Kittens. Have shots. To good home only. 314-8972.

Daniel Craig

Elizabeth D. Squire

One day in the mid-1800's, a stubborn man boarded a steamship as it neared Halifax, Nova Scotia. In his hands was a basket of carrier pigeons. In his coat pocket was hidden another pigeon. The man was Daniel Craig, and he wanted to be first with the news.

In the 1800's, no radios or telephones existed, and all the news from Europe came by steamship. The ships made their first North American stop in Nova Scotia. Then they sailed down to the large eastern cities of the United States.

Daniel Craig wanted to get stories to newspapers in Boston and New York before the steamships did. He had learned how pigeons could be trained to return to their home roosts with messages strapped to their legs. He decided these birds could be used to carry news.

So, with pigeons in hand, Craig would take a boat out to meet the ships from Europe before they arrived in Halifax. After boarding a ship, he would write up the most important news: wars which had started or ended; kings, queens, or heads of state who had come to power or died. Then he would attach his news report to the leg of a pigeon and send the bird flying off.

The pigeon would fly to its home on the roof of a newspaper office. The newspaper then bought and used Craig's news.

Some rival newspapers wanted to stop Craig. They tried to persuade the ships not to allow him to bring his birds on board. For this reason, Craig began carrying a bird in his pocket each time he boarded a ship.

Once, Craig and his basket of carrier pigeons boarded the ship of a strict captain named Byrie. Captain Byrie took Craig's basket of birds. He said that they would not be returned until the ship reached Boston. But Craig attached the news to the leg of his hidden bird. Then he went up on deck, stood right next to the captain, and released the bird.

The angry captain ran for his rifle and tried to shoot the bird. But by the time he could take aim and fire, the carrier pigeon was already a mile in the air. It was on its way to Boston. Craig again was first with the news.

When the rival newspapers found they could not beat Craig's news, they hired him. The rooftops of their buildings then became landing areas for pigeons.

Prior to this time, a new kind of printing press was invented. The old presses had been able to print only a few hundred pages an hour. The new press was a steam-driven press that could print 2,000 pages an hour. Later, it was improved so that it printed 4,000 pages an hour.

With the new press, newspapers made more money, and soon there was an increase in the number of new newspapers. Each wanted to get as many readers as possible. However, the cost of getting the news was still expensive. Boats were hired to meet ships in the harbor and rush the news to shore. Pony expresses were hired to carry the news overland.

Finally, in 1848, the six most important New York newspapers decided that an agency should be formed to collect the news and get it to the papers. The agency was called the *Associated Press*. Daniel Craig was hired to send the news from Halifax to the *AP*.

By the time Craig went to work for the *AP*, the telegraph had been developed. Poles carrying telegraph wires reached as far north as Portland, Maine. But there was only one wire for use in sending messages. The reporter who got to Portland first got his story through first. As always, Craig meant to be first.

Here's what he did. First, Craig's news reached shore at Halifax. There, an express rider was ready to gallop off to the Nova Scotia port town that was nearest Maine. A few miles

outside of this town, Craig placed a man with a cannon. The man would fire the cannon when the express rider was in sight. This sound signaled the captain of another steamship to get up steam and go to shore to pick up the news. The ship carried the news full steam down the coast of Maine to Portland and the single telegraph wire.

By 1849, the telegraph wires reached Halifax. Even then, Craig had to be clever. Another man wanted to sell foreign news, as Craig was doing. Once, this man managed to get to the telegraph wire in Halifax first and to block Craig's news. After that, Craig sent a friend to the telegraph office as soon as a steamship was sighted. The friend handed the operator a book and asked him to start sending the first chapter as AP "news" to New York. This "news" kept the wire busy until the "rest" of the AP news arrived from the ship. It was an expensive way to reserve the line, but Craig meant to be first.

Finally, one day in 1851, Craig received a telegram calling him to New York to see the publishers who employed him. The publishers asked Craig to become the general agent in charge of the *AP*. The *AP* had begun selling news to newspapers in many parts of the country. Thus, Craig now had to report a story in such a way as to make it useable by a Northern paper as well as a Southern paper. It also had to be useable by a Democratic-Party or a Republican-Party paper. Therefore, the *AP* news service had had to stick to the facts and get the facts as correct as possible.

Most newspapers at that time did not report the facts as accurately as possible. News stories were full of the opinions of the editors. They printed good news about the people they liked. They often published anything bad they could find about their enemies. They frequently failed to check the facts.

Craig made all his newspeople get the facts of a story exactly right. If they discovered a mistake, they had to send a second wire correcting it.

While he was the general agent of the *AP*, Craig saw many changes occur that helped to speed the news. One was the Atlantic cable, completed in 1866. This cable made it possible to receive news from across the ocean on the same day it occurred.

Craig left the *AP* in 1866 and started his own news agency. But he was not able to compete with the *AP* and soon retired from newsreporting.

Nevertheless, while Craig was in charge of the *AP*, the agency formed two important guides for news-gathering: get the news fast, and get the correct facts.

What's New?

Almost everyone likes to learn the latest news. One way to learn the latest news is by reading the newspaper. A newspaper informs you about important events. It also entertains you. A newspaper has many parts:

News articles give information about world, national, or local events. In the selection "What Do You Know About Newspapers?" you read news articles about an explorer reaching the North Pole, a governor approving a bill, a planned space flight, a circus performance, and a summer sports program.

Editorials are essays that tell the opinions of the newspaper's editors. In *The Daily Banner,* you read an editorial in which the editors gave reasons why Americans should use the metric system.

Letters to the Editor are written by people who want to express their opinions. In *The Daily Banner,* you read letters in which people told how they felt about litterbugs, the metric system, and the town's new traffic light.

Advertisements are notices written by store owners, manufacturers, and others. They tell about products or goods for sale or use. In *The Daily Banner,* you saw advertisements for a movie and a sale.

Classified Ads (or Advertisements) are placed by individuals or by businesses. They may announce job openings or items for sale. Some of the ads in *The Daily Banner* announced apartments for rent, musical instruments for sale, and jobs available for a babysitter, and a stock person.

A *weather report* gives the predicted weather for the day. Some reports give predictions for later days.

Cartoons and comics entertain the reader. A cartoon is usually one funny picture. Comics may be a series of pictures that tell a funny story.

Entertainment listings give information about TV and radio programs. They may also tell what movies are playing in town.

ACTIVITY A   On your paper, name the newspaper part that would answer each question.

1. Is it supposed to rain tomorrow?

2. What's on television tonight?

3. What was the score in yesterday's ball game?

4. Does anyone have a used trumpet for sale?

5. Is Winkles Store having a sale this week?

ACTIVITY B   On your paper, name the part of the newspaper that would give the following information.

1. The mayor takes a trip around the world.

2. Apartment for rent: 3 rooms, $350 a month.

3. Charlie Brown and Snoopy lose a ball game.

4. People give reasons for wanting a new park.

5. It will be sunny today and cloudy tonight.

6. Dress shoes at Shoe World are on sale: $15 a pair.

7. Business leaders meet to discuss world problems.

8. The editor explains the need to raise taxes.

RADIO

Before television, people used to listen to the radio. They listened to many kinds of programs for entertainment the way people watch television today. There were mysteries, spy stories, and westerns. And there were programs about science fiction and make-believe worlds.

While you listened to the radio, you might have heard Clark Kent change into Superman and take off after some robbers. How could you have heard him change into Superman? Well, the people who produced the radio shows made you hear it by using sound effects. The actors read their parts from the script. And the sound-effects people supplied the sounds needed. Using different props, they made the listener hear thunder crashing, bombs exploding, or horses running. They made whatever sound was necessary to make the program seem more realistic.

Radio also depended on the listener's imagination to make programs believable. When a character was described as a beautiful, young princess, that's what the audience imagined. It's like reading a book that has no pictures.

Here is a script from a radio show for young people. The program was *Let's Pretend.* It was very popular from 1930 to 1953.

Each week *Let's Pretend* dramatized a well-known story for young people. The script you are going to read is for "King Midas and the Golden Touch." It was first presented on February 12, 1944.

You will see that along with the parts for the characters, there is also a part for sound. Each time you see this part, there will be a suggestion for a sound effect that should be created in that place.

If you have a tape recorder in your classroom, you may wish to record the script with the sound effects. And then you can present your own *Let's Pretend* show.

KING MIDAS AND THE GOLDEN TOUCH

Nila Mack

CHARACTERS:
Announcer
King Midas
Catalan, the king's advisor
Professor Messor, the king's scientist
Marygold, the king's daughter
Aurum, the spirit of gold
Landers, the king's servant
Leandra, the king's maid

Announcer: Once upon a time, there lived a very rich king whose name was Midas. He had a little daughter whom he named Marygold. He'd chosen this name especially because it had *gold* in it. Gold was the thing he liked best in all the world—next to the little princess herself. King Midas had great quantities of gold in his treasure room, but he was always trying to figure out ways to get more. Right now he's talking to his advisor, Catalan.

Sound: *Happy music* (5 seconds then fade out)

Midas: War...that's one way to get gold, Catalan. But if I declared war on some country, some of my soldiers would surely perish.

Catalan: There are plenty of kings who wouldn't let that stop them. You have a heart of gold, Your Majesty. You don't want your subjects to suffer.

Midas: Heart of gold! Can I put *that* in my treasure room? Can I weigh it? Feel it in my hand?

Catalan: Well, no, sire, but . . .

Midas: And that scientist, Professor Messor! Is he making any progress turning brass into gold?

Catalan: He's trying, Your Majesty. He's always working with those chemicals and potions. So far, there's been nothing, but . . .

Sound: *Dull explosion* (drop a heavy book on the desk)

Catalan (*as explosion dies out*): . . . explosions.

Sound: *Door opens, hurried steps* (hold shoes in your hand and use them to make running sounds on the table)

Professor: I'm sorry, Your Majesty. It was just a slight mistake.

Midas: I hope you weren't hurt.

Professor: No, Your Majesty.

Midas: And I take it you're no closer to finding a magic formula for making gold than you were yesterday—or a year ago.

Professor: Sire, we seek to unlock the riddle that has puzzled people for centuries. We can't hope to find an answer quickly.

Midas: I'm beginning to wonder if we can find the answer in a lifetime.

Professor: I'll get back to work at once, sire. *(Fading)* Have faith, Your Highness!

Marygold *(fading in):* Are you busy now, Father?

Midas: Never too busy for a "good morning" from my little Marygold. How are you today?

Marygold: Fine, Father. I've brought you a present from the garden! Buttercups and daffodils!

Midas: Very pretty, little one . . . the color of gold. Just think. If they really were gold, they'd be worth a king's ransom.

Marygold: But Father, you don't need to be ransomed from anybody. What use is more gold?

Midas: Child, you talk of things you don't understand. Now run along and play.

Marygold: Couldn't you come out with me for a while?

Midas: No, Marygold. It's time now for me to go to the treasure house with Catalan. I have to count my gold, little daughter. It's for you I'm collecting it. . . . So you'll always have everything you want.

Marygold: The only thing I want is to spend more time with you.

Midas: Just wait, Marygold. When I've finally collected enough, we'll be together all the time.

Marygold (sighs): It just seems like you'll never have enough. (Fading) Goodbye, Father. Goodbye, Catalan.

Sound: Fading footsteps

Catalan: Goodbye, little princess.

Sound: Door closes

Midas: Well, then. Come along to the underground vaults and help me count what's there.

Sound: Happy music (5 seconds)

Sound: Clink of metal bowls

Catalan (fading in): That's ten thousand and fifteen golden bowls.

49

Midas: And how many bags of gold did you say?

Catalan: Two million, sire.

Midas: A goodly number, but it's not enough.
All right, Catalan. Take those tally sheets into
the next room and come back as soon as
you have the totals.

Catalan *(fading):* Yes, sire.

Sound: *Fading footsteps, door shuts*

Midas: Golden bowls, bars of gold, gold in bags,
and gold in boxes. But it's not enough. It's
hardly a handful compared to what I might
have. Oh, I want all the gold in the world!
All of it!

Sound: *Tambourine shakes*

Midas *(startled):* What was that?

Sound: *Cymbals crash*

Aurum: Greetings, King Midas.

Midas: Who is this? Is it a dream?

Aurum: No, King Midas, it is not a dream. I am
Aurum, the Spirit of Gold.

Midas: The Spirit of Gold! No wonder you appear
so golden. Why have you come to me?

Aurum: I know that you have much gold, King Midas. But I know that you do not think you have enough. What would satisfy you, my king? Perhaps I might help you.

Midas: You might? Oh, my, I'd better think of a really worthwhile wish. I . . . I . . . I have it! Aurum, Spirit of Gold, I wish that everything that I touch be turned to gold!

Aurum: Are you quite sure this will make you happy?

Midas: How could it fail?

Aurum: Very well. Tomorrow, with the first rays of the rising sun, you will find yourself gifted with . . . THE GOLDEN TOUCH.

Sound: *Tambourine shakes, then cymbals crash*

Midas: He's gone. Can what he promised be true? Tomorrow at sunrise will I have THE GOLDEN TOUCH!

Sound: *Happy music (5 seconds), rooster crows in distance* (have someone crow like a rooster)

Midas *(yawns):* Oh that roo . . . oh my goodness! Today's the day. Landers! Confound that man . . . never around when you want him! Landers!

Sound: *Running steps fade in*

Landers *(fading in):* Sire! Is something wrong?

Midas: Of course not. Why aren't you properly dressed?

Landers: But, sire . . . it isn't even daylight yet. The sun . . .

Midas: Never mind. Let me touch something. The bell cord! It would look very fine if it were gold.

Sound: *Little bells ring in distance five times*

Leandra *(fading in, breathless):* Yes, Your Majesty?

Midas: It didn't work. Why are you two staring at me?

Landers: Sire, you've never been up before the sun before.

Midas: The sun isn't up yet. That's what it is. All right, girl. You can run along now. Landers, fix my shaving things.

Sound: *Water splashing* (splash water in a large bowl)

Midas: I'll busy myself shaving. Any sign of the sun yet, Landers?

Landers: It's just barely visible at the horizon.

Midas: Soon, soon! I'll know soon.

Sound: *Splash is suddenly followed by ring of metal* (splash water and hit empty metal bowl with wooden spoon)

Midas: By all the powers, it's happened. Landers! Look! The water's turned to gold!

Landers: Sire?

Midas: Bring me the china pitcher!

Sound: *Pitcher rattles followed by ring of metal* (tap two china cups together and hit empty metal bowl with wooden spoon)

Landers: What's happening here?

Midas: Can't you see what's happening? My clothes, Landers! Bring them to me quickly.

Landers: Your shirt and trousers, sire.

Sound: *Rattle of aluminum foil*

Midas: My shirt and trousers are gold!

Landers: Heavens above us!

Midas: My boots, Landers. Bring me my boots!

Sound: *Clump of boot followed by ring of metal*

Midas: Gold boots. But is it real gold? The scientist! Professor Messor! He will know. I'll show my boots to him right now. Oh, wait until Marygold sees what I can do.

Sound: *Running footsteps with a clanging sound*

Midas *(panting):* Professor Messor! Look at my boots!

Professor: Why, they are gold, sire.

Midas: Real gold, Professor? Test them. Scratch them. Do whatever you do!

Professor: I don't have to do anything. I can see they are real gold. Pure gold, but . . .

Midas: It's happened! It's happened! Anything I touch turns to gold!

Professor: But, sire, how? . . .

Midas: You don't believe I can do it? Well, just look. I'll pick up this wooden stool.

Sound: *Scrape of wood followed by clang of metal*

Midas: It's pure gold. I have only to touch anything, and it's pure gold! It's the golden touch!

Professor: You have only to touch things and they're transformed! What will I do? I've been working my whole life to change brass to gold. What do I do now?

Midas: I don't know, Professor. But I know what I'm going to do. I'm going to find Marygold and show her what I can do.

Sound: *Hurrying steps*

Midas *(fading out):* Marygold! Marygold!

Sound: *Happy music (10 seconds)*

Sound: *Clink of china being set down*

Leandra: His breakfast is here, but he is not.
Oh, what is going on this morning?

Landers: Come here, Leandra. Look out the
window and see for yourself.

Leandra: Why he's racing from flower to flower.
And he's touching each one.

Landers: And laughing like a crazy man. But he's
coming this way now. You'll soon see for
yourself.

Leandra: What will I see?

Landers: Shhh—here he comes.

Sound: *Door opens*

Midas *(fading in, excited)*: Marygold? Is she here?

Landers: No, Your Majesty. She just went out into
the garden.

Midas: I must have just missed her. Well, she's
sure to be along for breakfast very soon. I'm
starving. Bring on the eggs, Leandra.

Sound: *China being set down on table*

Midas: Ah eggs! I'm starving.

Sound: *Metal dropping on plate* (drop coins into
empty metal bowl)

Midas: Ow!

Leandra: Your Majesty! What happened?

Midas: I've burned my fingers to the bone on that hunk of molten metal—that's what! My goodness! I turned that egg into gold. *(Frightened a little)* But what am I going to eat? I'm hungry! Will every bite of food turn into gold before I can. . .?

> (MARYGOLD *fades in crying*)

Marygold, what is it?

Marygold: Oh, Father, a dreadful thing has happened. My garden—my beautiful garden is ruined. Something awful has happened to every flower.

Midas: Not *awful*, Marygold.

Marygold: All the flowers are hard metal. There's no fragrance. The petals scratch me. What could have happened?

Midas: Marygold, don't cry. Look! Isn't this a beautiful golden rose?

Marygold: It isn't. I hate it that way.

Midas: Marygold! Please, dear! Oh, I hate to see you so unhappy. . . . Come here to your father.

Marygold (*sobbing*): Oh, Father, change them back.

Midas: Come here, dear.

Sound: *Cling of a big metal object being tapped, then thud of a heavy object being set down*

Midas (*shocked*): Marygold! What have I done! My daughter has turned to gold!

Sound: *Funeral music* (10 seconds)

Midas: I shall be in my room all afternoon, Landers. Please see that I am not disturbed.

Landers: Yes, Your Majesty.

Sound: *Fading footsteps, door closes*

Midas: Great Aurum, I would do anything to have my little girl alive. I would give everything I have.

Sound: *Tambourine shakes*

Midas (*pleadingly*): Aurum, do you hear?

Sound: *Cymbals crash*

Aurum: Well, Midas?

Midas: Aurum? You're here. Oh, Spirit of Gold, help me.

Aurum: King Midas with the golden touch. How can *you* need help?

Midas: The golden touch has cost me everything that was worthwhile.

Aurum: Then you have made a discovery?

58

Midas: Oh, I have learned too well . . . and too late.

Aurum: Let me see. Which of these two things do you think is worth more—the golden touch or a crust of bread?

Midas: A piece of bread is worth all the gold on earth.

Aurum: The golden touch or your little daughter?

Midas: Oh, my child. Restore her to me! Help me, Aurum. Have pity! Help me!

Aurum: You are wiser than you were, my king. At last you seem to see that the commonest things are more valuable than riches. Tell me, do you really wish to be rid of your golden touch?

Midas: Oh, yes. With all my heart.

Aurum: Then go to the river that glides past the bottom of your garden. Plunge into it. Take with you a vase and fill it with river water. If your promise is true, if you have really cleansed your soul of greed for gold, you will be able to undo this tragedy.

Midas: And bring Marygold back to life?

Aurum: Sprinkle the water over her, and she will be restored. If you are honest within yourself, she will have no memory of what has happened.

Midas: Aurum, with all my heart I thank you.

Sound: *Cymbals crash*

Leandra: Where was he going when he rushed out of here with that vase, Landers?

Landers: "To the river," he said. Oh, my poor king. No wonder he is distraught. Look at the little girl princess. Just look at her.

Leandra: A golden statue. The poor child.

Landers: Shh. Here he comes back again. The vase is full of water!

Sound: *Footsteps hurry in*

Midas: Landers and Leandra. See to it that whatever happens in the next few moments you keep to yourselves. I ask this, not as your king, but as a father who loves his child.

Landers and Leandra: Yes, Your Majesty.

Midas: And now, Spirit of Gold, if honesty is the test, let my child be restored.

Sound: *Swoosh of water* (empty pitcher of water all at once into empty metal bowl)

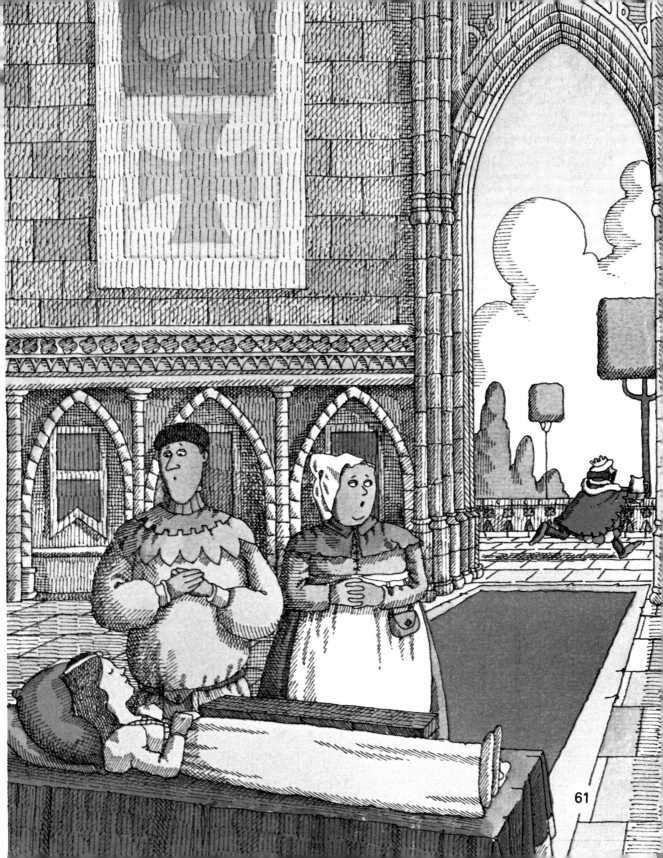

61

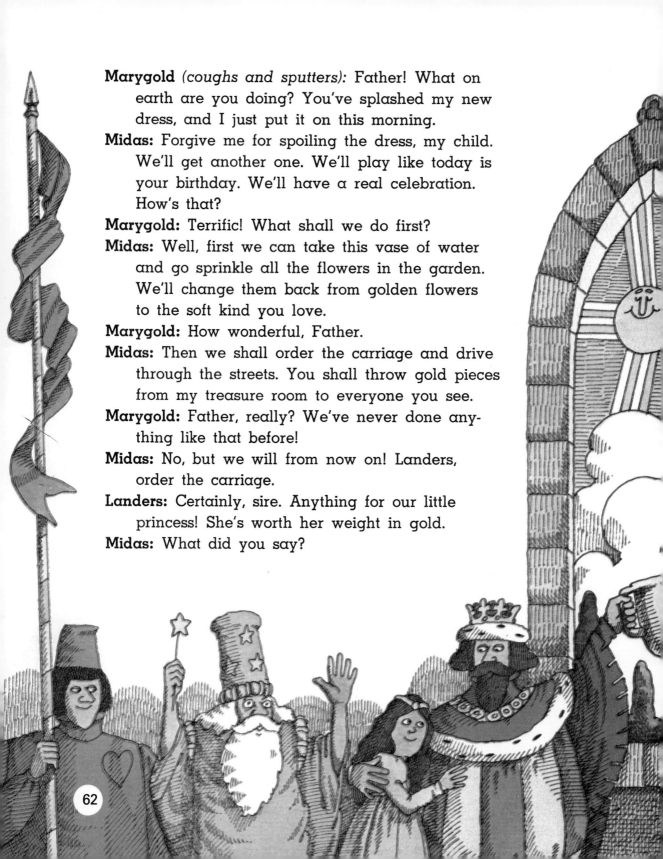

Marygold *(coughs and sputters):* Father! What on earth are you doing? You've splashed my new dress, and I just put it on this morning.

Midas: Forgive me for spoiling the dress, my child. We'll get another one. We'll play like today is your birthday. We'll have a real celebration. How's that?

Marygold: Terrific! What shall we do first?

Midas: Well, first we can take this vase of water and go sprinkle all the flowers in the garden. We'll change them back from golden flowers to the soft kind you love.

Marygold: How wonderful, Father.

Midas: Then we shall order the carriage and drive through the streets. You shall throw gold pieces from my treasure room to everyone you see.

Marygold: Father, really? We've never done anything like that before!

Midas: No, but we will from now on! Landers, order the carriage.

Landers: Certainly, sire. Anything for our little princess! She's worth her weight in gold.

Midas: What did you say?

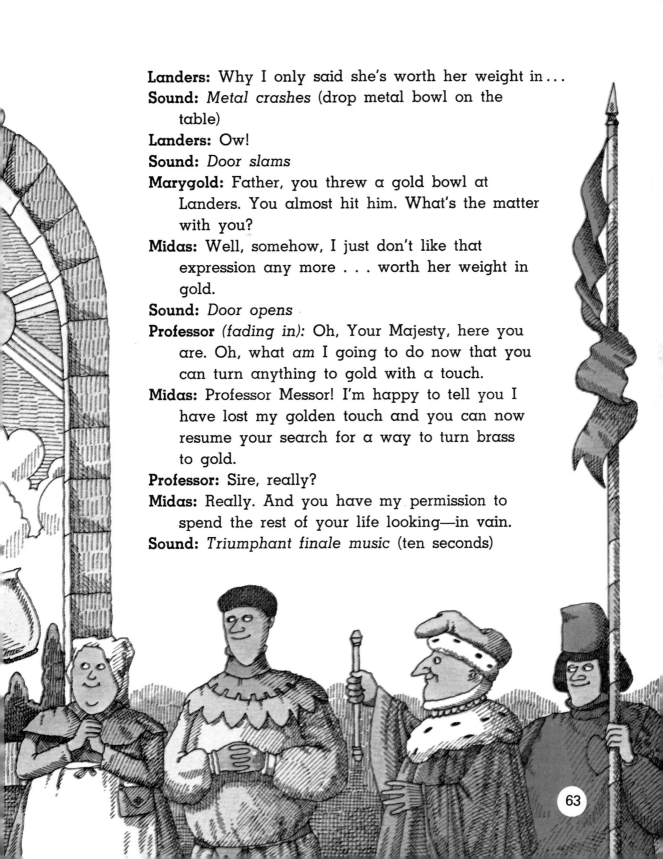

Landers: Why I only said she's worth her weight in . . .

Sound: *Metal crashes* (drop metal bowl on the table)

Landers: Ow!

Sound: *Door slams*

Marygold: Father, you threw a gold bowl at Landers. You almost hit him. What's the matter with you?

Midas: Well, somehow, I just don't like that expression any more . . . worth her weight in gold.

Sound: *Door opens*

Professor *(fading in):* Oh, Your Majesty, here you are. Oh, what *am* I going to do now that you can turn anything to gold with a touch.

Midas: Professor Messor! I'm happy to tell you I have lost my golden touch and you can now resume your search for a way to turn brass to gold.

Professor: Sire, really?

Midas: Really. And you have my permission to spend the rest of your life looking—in vain.

Sound: *Triumphant finale music* (ten seconds)

ZOOMING IN ON ZOOM

A. Whitney

Have you ever stopped to think about what goes into preparing a television show? We thought it would be interesting to find out, so we went to station WGBH in Boston. That's where the program *Zoom* is taped each week. We chose *Zoom* because the material for the show is written almost entirely by the youngsters who watch it. There have been many programs for young people since television became popular. But *Zoom* is the first to be written by young viewers.

Like all television shows, *Zoom* started out as an idea. Chris Sarson, who has worked in television for many years, wanted to give young people a chance to have a show that was really their own. It took three years of work and planning before the first *Zoom* program went on the air in January 1971. Since then, *Zoom* has been viewed on television stations all over the country.

Most television shows have script writers who write the material that will be used. The "script writers" for *Zoom* are the show's viewers. They supply all the material used on *Zoom* except the musical production numbers. These are prepared by a musical director and a choreographer.

Each day between 1,500 and 20,000 letters arrive at the *Zoom* mailroom. Youngsters from all over the country send riddles, games, plays, recipes, experiments, and stories that they would like to see presented on the show. Many fan letters are received in the mailroom, too. A staff of volunteers reads through each letter and decides which ones contain material that might be presented on the show.

The producer, director, and editors of *Zoom* read through the material sent them from the mailroom and decide which things will be used.

The seven youngsters who perform on *Zoom* each week are called "Zoomers." They rehearse after school two afternoons a week at the WGBH studio.

Like most television programs, *Zoom* is not performed at the time that you see it. *Zoom* is recorded on video tape. That is why the same program can be seen at different times and on different days all over the country.

On a typical taping day, the production schedule for *Zoom* begins several hours before the Zoomers arrive from school.

At one o'clock the people who work the lights arrive. They have to make sure that all of the lights are working, and that they have the lights they need in the right places.

At two o'clock another group of people arrives at the studio. They check the three television cameras to be used that day. Then they place the microphones where they belong and make sure that the scenery to be used is all together and looks right.

By 3:30 the Zoomers arrive at the studio. They rehearse their musical number a little more to smooth out any rough spots. While this is going

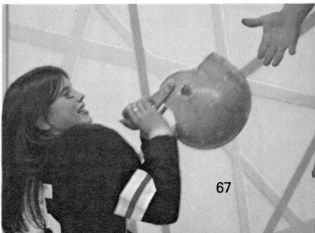

on, *Zoom's* director rehearses the camera crew so that they know which cameras will be used at certain points during the show. The lighting director makes sure that the proper lighting has been arranged.

At four o'clock the cameras are ready to roll! The first item to be taped is a musical number. The Zoomers take their places. Lights, camera, action. The number has been taped. But wait. A couple of Zoomers were out of step. Better try it again. The Zoomers go through the number again before the cameras. It usually takes between two and six "takes" to get a final product that is perfect.

As the Zoomers dance, they move their lips to look like they are singing. But they aren't. The song is taped separately from the dance so the Zoomers sound clear and not out of breath. This song tape is then played along with the dance tape so it looks like the Zoomers are singing and dancing at the same time. This way of taping is common in television.

At five o'clock, the Zoomers and the crew eat supper. They still have several hours to go before this week's production work will be finished.

69

At six o'clock the Zoomers and the crew are back in the studio. While the performers rehearse the play they will tape, the crew sets up the scenery needed for the play.

Seven o'clock. Time to tape the play. The Zoomers take their positions. Lights, camera, action. A "take" is made. Then, another and maybe another, just to be sure.

At 8 o'clock the crew and cast take a break. But not for long. Because at 8:15 everybody is back at work again. There are many other things to be taped: riddles, games, experiments, and recipes, to name a few. The cameras and people work until 9:30. Then, between 9:30 and 10 o'clock, the cameras and lights are unplugged and the scenery is removed. In the morning, the studio may be used to tape a different show.

The day in the studio is over. About three hours of tape have been made. But there is still one more step before *Zoom* can go on the air.

This next step in preparing the television program is called editing. Editing is the way in which the best scenes from the video tape are selected for the final production.

In editing, the pieces that were taped are viewed, and it is decided which ones will actually be used on a telecast. Only one "take" of the musical number and the play will be used. And, for example, some of the games or experiments that have been taped may be shortened. So although the cameras have worked for about three hours, the final product is a *Zoom* program thirty minutes long. So there you are. Now *Zoom* is ready to go on the air.

Next time you turn on your favorite television program, think of all the steps and the people that are needed to produce one show. Now you know it's not as easy as it looks.

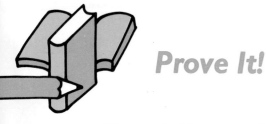

Prove It!

You probably see and hear many advertisements each day. They are on television and on radio. They appear in newspapers and magazines. To be a smart buyer, you must study ads carefully. First, decide if each statement is a fact or an opinion.

A *fact* is a statement that can be proven true or false. You can check facts by looking in reference books or by seeing for yourself if they are true. The statement, "A box of *Golden Pancake Mix* costs thirty-nine cents," is a fact. You can check its truth by looking at the box.

An *opinion* is a statement that tells someone's belief about something. It cannot be proven true or false. The statement, *"Golden Pancakes* taste good," is an opinion. To some people, this statement may be true. Other people may not agree that *Golden Pancakes* taste good.

ACTIVITY A   **Read each statement. Write Fact if the statement is a fact. Write Opinion if it is an opinion.**

1. *Dento* toothpaste comes in three different sizes.
2. *Dento* toothpaste has a delicious flavor.
3. This toothpaste smells good, too.
4. *Dento* toothpaste is selling at halfprice this week.
5. *Dento* contains a compound called *hexifloride.*
6. The design on the tube is beautiful.
7. The Dento Company also sells toothbrushes.
8. The tube is printed in white and blue.
9. *Dento* is the best selling toothpaste in the country.

An advertisement can offer two types of opinions. *Personal opinion* is a belief based on one person's feelings about something. *Expert testimony* is the opinion of an expert in the field. You should trust expert testimony more than you trust personal opinion.

Suppose you saw two car advertisements. In one ad, a movie star said that a car was safe. In the other ad, a driving teacher said that a car was safe. You should trust the second opinion more than the first. The driving teacher is an expert in handling cars.

ACTIVITY B Imagine that each statement below appears in an advertisement. Read each statement. Then read the descriptions of the two people who might have made the statement. On your paper, write the description of the person whose opinion is the most trustworthy.

1. *Growrite* vitamins are good for you.
   a. a doctor of medicine
   b. a doctor of engineering

2. *Pepso* chewing gum is fine for your teeth.
   a. a famous baseball player
   b. a dentist

3. *Dudso* detergent is best for washing clothes.
   a. the owner of a laundry
   b. the owner of a shoe store

4. *Tracto* tires are dependable in bad weather.
   a. a taxi driver
   b. a well-known comedian

5. *Saf-T* toys are the safest toys for babies.
   a. a small child
   b. a nursery-school director

May 1, 1972

Dear Senator Moss,

My name is Dawn A Kurth. I am 11 years old and in 5th grade at Meadowlane Elementary school in Melbourne Florida. Recently I was selected by my teachers to do a project in the Talented Student Program in Brevard.

My project is the study of deceptive advertising towards parents through children. Recently I have received a copy of your bill and I read It with interest.

I thought you might be interested in seeing a survey I made on children's reaction towards T.V. commercials (I inclued the survey in with this letter)

I recently met Mr. Robert B. Choate and he told me your committee would be holding hearings about advertising and children in May. I was wondering If you would like me to come and give a child's veiw of the whole thing and tell the committee about my survey.

Thank You   Dawn A. Kurth

Commercials and you

Dawn Kurth

When Dawn Kurth was in the fifth grade, she decided that TV commercials were often misleading and even harmful.

Dawn drew up a questionnaire about TV advertising. She wanted to see if other youngsters shared her views. She learned that many youngsters buy products advertised on TV to get free gifts. And she learned that many youngsters are very disappointed with the gifts they receive.

Then Dawn heard that the United States Senate was holding a special hearing about TV commercials. She went to Washington to tell her story. You will read about it on the following pages.

My name is Dawn Ann Kurth. On May 31, 1972,
I testified before the Senate Commerce Committee.
I told the Committee about a project I had done. I
had studied TV commercials that are aimed at kids.
I thought my appearance at the hearing would
be the end of my project. But as it has turned out, it
was the beginning of the most exciting thing that has
ever happened to me.

It all started last fall. Our school began a new
program. The program gave kids a chance to do a
project in any field they wanted. I wanted to do a
project that would maybe help the world be a little
better for people. At the same time, my sister Martha
had a problem. She had asked my mother to buy a
certain brand of cereal. It had a free record on the
back of the box. My mother finally bought the cereal.
But when Martha got the record, it wouldn't work.
She was really upset. She asked my mother to buy
the cereal again to get another record that might work
better.

I began to think about what was happening. It really made me mad. I had seen the commercial that advertised the record. It really worked well on TV. People were laughing and dancing to it. I knew it wasn't right that my sister had been fooled. I felt that maybe lots of other kids had the same problem. That is when I decided to investigate commercials shown on kid's TV programs.

The first thing I did was to sit down and keep a record of all the commercials shown on Saturday morning. There were so many, my mother had to help me write them down. Then I began to think about the messages that the commercials were giving to kids. Many of the commercials were misleading or told kids things that didn't make sense.

Some of the commercials were dangerous. They were advertising vitamin pills by telling kids how good they were. They were comparing vitamins to chocolate cookies. I knew that if my three-year-old sister were to get a bottle of those pills, she would eat them all. I felt it was wrong to advertise something to kids that said on the bottle, "Keep out of the reach of children."

My next step was to find out if kids really believed the commercials. I surveyed 1,540 kids. I tried to find out how they felt about commercials. When I got the results of my survey, I knew that TV commercials influence kids a lot. So I decided to do what I could to make them better and more truthful.

I began writing letters. I wrote to anyone I thought would help. That is how I heard about the Senate Commerce Committee hearing. I wrote to Senator Moss. I asked if the senators would like me to come to the hearing. I said I would like to give a kid's view of television ads directed at kids.

I wrote to the committee. But I really didn't expect to be asked to come to Washington. Then a few days later, my mother got a phone call from the committee. The committee was interested in what I had to say. My mother was very excited. She couldn't wait for me to come home. My mother came to school to tell me!

My mother and I went to Washington the day
before the hearing. The next morning, we walked to
the Senate Office Building. That's where the hearing
was going to be held. In the hearing room, the
networks were setting up TV cameras. Reporters were
running in and out. Some of them talked to me. And
some were surprised to hear that I was going to
testify. I was the second witness. I didn't hear too
much of what the first one said.

Then my name was called. The senators sat on a raised platform at the front of the room. The witness table was in front of them. There was a typist taking down everything that was said. All the testimony was going into the *Congressional Record*. I sat at the witness table.

Here is some of my testimony:

To begin my project, I kept a record of the number of commercials shown on Saturday morning TV shows. There were twenty-five commercials during one hour, from 8:00 to 9:00 A.M. This is not counting ads for shows coming up or public service ads. I found there were only ten to twelve commercials during shows my parents like to watch. For the first time, I really began to think about what commercials were saying. I had always listened to them before. And many times, I had asked my mother to buy certain products I had seen. But now I was really listening. And I was thinking about what was said.

One type of commercial advertises a free bonus gift if you buy a certain product. The commercial tells about the bonus gift. It says nothing about the product they want you to buy. Many times, the bonus gift is worthless junk or isn't in the package. I wrote to the TV networks. They told me it costs about $4,000 for a thirty-second commercial. Many of those ads appeared four times in each hour. Why would any company spend $15,000 or $20,000 an hour to advertise worthless junk?

These ads I consider misleading. But others I feel are dangerous.

Some vitamin ads say their vitamins taste "yummy."

Let's say my mother were to buy those vitamins. If my little sister found them, I am sure she would eat them as if they were candy.

I do not know a lot about nutrition. But I do know that my mother tries to keep us from eating so many sweets. She says they are bad for our teeth. Our dentist says so, too. If they are bad, why are companies allowed to make children want them by advertising?

I know the people who make these commercials are not bad. I know the commercials pay for TV shows. And I like to watch TV. I just think that it would be as easy to produce a good commercial as a bad one. If nothing good can be said about a product that is the truth, perhaps it should not be sold in the first place.

I do not know all the ways to write a good commercial. But I think commercials would be good if they taught kids something. Something that was true and maybe educational. They could teach about good health. They could tell kids about where food is grown.

People who write commercials are much smarter than I. They should be able to think of many ways to write a commercial that tells the truth about a product. They should not tell kids to eat a cereal because it is the world's sweetest or because it's "shaped like fun." What shape is fun, anyway?

I also think kids should not be bribed by commercials telling of wonderful free bonus gifts.

Kids should not be told to eat a certain product because a well-known hero does.

I think vitamin companies should be more careful. They should never be allowed to say vitamins are delicious or yummy. They should not make the children think vitamins are candy. Perhaps these commercials could teach children the dangers of taking drugs. Or they could teach children to tell a grownup if they find a bottle of pills. And they should tell kids never to eat the medicine.

I want to thank the Commerce Committee and especially Chairman Moss, for letting me appear. When I leave Washington, D.C., I will remember for the rest of my life that people do care what kids think. I know I could have led a protest about commercials through our shopping center. People would have laughed at me. Or they would have thought I needed a good spanking. Or they would have wondered what kind of parents I had that would let me protest. Instead I gathered my information and wrote letters to anyone I thought would listen. Many of them didn't listen. But some did. That is why I am here today. Because some people cared about what I thought. Now I can tell all the kids in America that when they see a wrong that needs to be right, they shouldn't just forget about it. They should not just hope it will go away. They should begin to do what they can to change it. People will listen. I know, because you're here listening to me.

Thank you.

After I finished testifying, the senator called a short recess. A lot of reporters came over to me. They asked me what I wanted to be when I grew up and things like that. There were two more witnesses. Then the hearing was over.

After lunch I met some more senators. We spent the rest of the afternoon touring the Capitol. Then we watched the news on TV. When they talked about the hearing, I was very happy. I knew a lot of people would be watching. Maybe some of them would write letters to their senators or representatives in congress about ads that fool kids.

That night I really slept well. In fact I overslept.
I nearly missed being on a TV morning news program. It
was my first time in a TV studio. I was very busy looking
around. I almost forgot to talk.

After that we visited the senator from Florida and our
representative in congress. Next I visited the Federal
Trade Commission, the FTC. I was very happy to do that.
The people there have the power to correct much of what
is wrong with TV ads. They said they were glad that I came.
They wished everyone would tell them about problems
they have with ads. This is the best way they have of
finding out what needs to be investigated.

When we left the FTC, it was almost time to go to the airport. I was anxious to get home. I wanted to tell the rest of my family about everything that had happened.

Finally the plane landed in Florida. There were lots of reporters and photographers waiting for me. My family was there. My fifth-grade teacher, the principal of my school, and members of the school board were there. And lots of friends were there. I can honestly say it was the happiest moment of my life.

The next day was Friday. I went to school. We didn't do too much studying. Everybody wanted to hear about my trip. All the kids were really interested in everything that had happened. Most of them would like to see ads made better. But some of them are worried.

They are afraid that, if companies stop advertising, we won't have any TV shows. I told them that companies didn't have to stop advertising. They should just make their ads more truthful. And they should give kids useful information. Then kids can make wise choices before they buy something. I think this is important. Kids should learn to be wise consumers.

Since the hearing, I have been on several radio and TV shows. And there have been a lot of things written in the paper about me. It is always exciting and a lot of fun when I'm on a show. But it hasn't changed me. Everyone who knows me treats me just the same. And that is how I like it. Most grownups ask me what I'm going to do next. I think they are happy a kid cares about what is going on. I have received dozens of letters. Most of them are from adults thanking me for my stand. They say they feel the same way I do. Because of all the letters and support, I'm going to keep working for better TV ads. Well, I would keep working for better ads even if I didn't get any support. I think what I'm doing is right. But encouragement from other kids and their parents makes it a lot easier.

In advertising, language is used in two ways. It is used *to state facts* about a product. It is also used *to persuade people* to buy the product.

Here is an example of the way language is used to state facts in an advertisement:

Garden Juice is good for you. It is made from carrots, tomatoes, and celery. A glass of Garden Juice supplies you with Vitamins A and D.

Here is an example of the way language in advertising is used to persuade people to buy something:

Drinking Garden Juice will make you first in your class. If you drink Garden Juice, you'll soon be stronger and healthier than you are now.

Now read the advertisement below. Find the sentences that state facts about the product. Then find the sentences that are used to persuade people to buy the product.

Mighty Milk is the best milk in the world. It is rich in Vitamin D. If you drink Mighty Milk, you will become the best player on your team. Mighty Milk is always fresh. It is delivered each day from a near-by dairy.

AT HOME IN THE FUTURE

Alma Whitney

A telephone small enough to wear on your wrist? A trip to the library without leaving your home? A medical examination without a doctor or nurse in the room?

These ideas may seem strange to you. But today work is being done in communication systems that may turn these ideas into realities within your lifetime.

Let's pretend that we can visit the twenty-first century. We will visit a boy named Peter Smith. He has already awakened this morning. But he is not feeling too well.

Mrs. Smith, Peter's mother, wants the doctor to see Peter. That is, it would be a good idea for the doctor to *listen* to Peter. Mrs. Smith brings a set of wires to Peter's bedside. These wires are called sensors. She places one sensor in his mouth and one on his chest. She puts another one around his wrist and one on his forehead. Then she plugs the sensors into a wall outlet. She says the code "TCP. " This means *telephone call placed.* A little light flashes on the wall. This indicates that the Smith's wireless telephone is ready to accept a call.

Mrs. Smith says "2478." That's the doctor's phone number.

From a speaker on the wall the doctor's voice says, "Good morning."

"Good morning, Dr. Cooper," answers Mrs. Smith. "Peter isn't feeling too well this morning. I've hooked him up to the sensors. I wonder if you can examine him now."

"Sure," the doctor's voice says over the speaker. "Well, he doesn't appear to have any fever. And his pulse rate is fine. Now, breathe deeply, Peter."

Peter breathes deeply.

"Just a little congestion in the chest," announces the doctor. "A little cold. Better stay inside today. And take it easy."

"Thank you, Doctor," says Mrs. Smith. "TCC (telephone call complete)." The light on the wall turns off. The phone call and examination are finished.

"Peter," says Mrs. Smith, "as long as you have to stay home, why don't you shop? You could pick out your new bicycle. Your birthday's only two weeks away."

"Great," Peter answers.

To shop for the bicycle, Peter and his mother and father sit in front of one of the visionphones. There are several in their house.

*Here is a business executive
using a picturephone.*

"TCP," says Peter. The word *ready* flashes on the screen of the visionphone.

"Do you know the number of the bicycle section at the merchandise center?" Mr. Smith asks Peter.

"Sure, Dad. It's 7752," Peter answers, loudly enough so that the call will go through.

"Eastwood Bicycle Shop," a voice says. "May we help you?"

Peter answers. "I'd like to see your line of ten-speed, two wheelers."

In the next few moments, pictures of many models of the bicycles are flashed on the screen of the Smith's visionphone. The price of each bike is also shown. After the last picture, a voice asks, "Is there a particular model that you wish to see again?"

"I'd like to see models 3 and 6," Peter answers. Pictures of models 3 and 6 are shown on the screen. A voice explains the features.

"I think number 6 is the one I really like," Peter tells his parents.

"Do you wish to place an order at this time?" asks a voice.

"Not just yet," says Mr. Smith. "My son's birthday isn't for two weeks. Thank you. TCC."

In the future, messages will be speeded through space by lasers like this one.

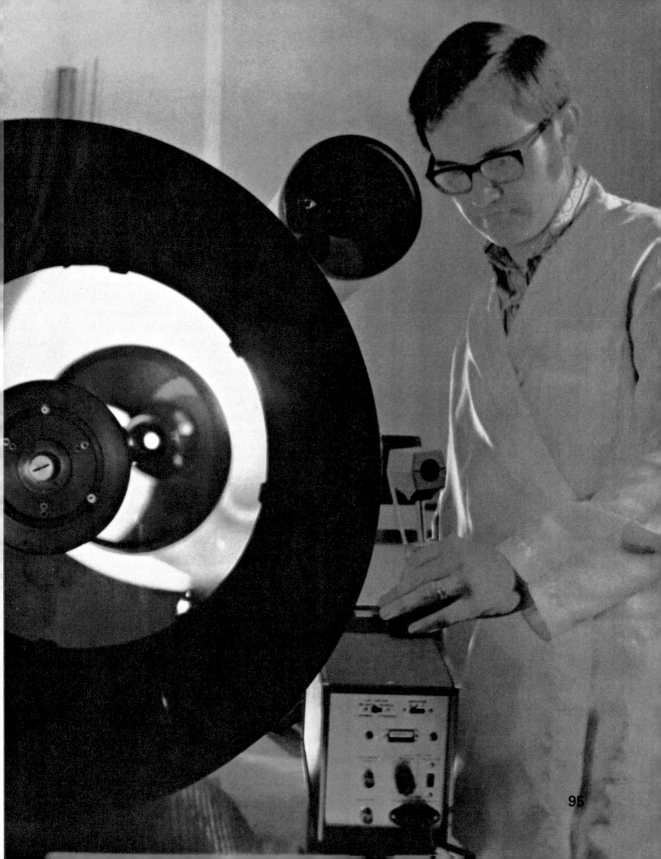

The visionphone shuts off.

The shopping is finished. Peter's parents tell Peter they have to go out for a little while. "Why don't you visit the library while we're gone," Peter's dad suggests. "I know they have some new books about basketball."

Peter goes to one of the visionphones. He places a call to the library. He asks to see one of the new books on basketball.

The title, *Basketball Giants*, appears on the screen. "Turn," says Peter. The first page of the book appears on the screen. Peter has read about thirty pages of it. Then he hears his mother's voice coming through a speaker on the wall. Peter turns off the visionphone. He says hello to his mother.

"Where are you?" he adds.

"We're driving on the freeway," Mrs. Smith says. "This is taking a little more time than we thought. Better get some lunch for yourself."

"What are you doing?" Peter asks.

"We'll explain later," she says.

Peter goes to the kitchen. He thinks about what he would like to have for lunch. Pizza! That sounds like just the thing to have for lunch on a day when you're home with a cold. Peter walks over to the menu selector. He presses a button marked *p*. A drawer containing recipes that begin with that letter slides out of a cabinet. Peter pulls out the recipe for pizza. He drops it into the meal-maker. He turns a dial on the meal-maker to *1*, meaning one portion.

While the meal-maker prepares the pizza, Peter takes a look at his treehouse. He's building it in the backyard. He switches on his home television camera and presses a button marked *yard*. Looking at the TV screen on the wall, he sees that the treehouse is in fine shape.

This city of the future will house 3000 people on ten acres of an 860 acre site.

It's just waiting for him to do some more work on it. Maybe tomorrow.

Beep, beep, beep. Lunch is ready. Peter returns to the meal-maker just in time to greet his pizza. It is coming out through a slot in the side of the machine.

The pizza is delicious. It really hits the spot. Peter is feeling much better now. He thinks he'll be well enough to go to school tomorrow. Thinking of school, Peter remembers that there is supposed to be a math test tomorrow. It is a math test for which he could use some studying. It's nice and quiet in the Smith's house now. A perfect time to study.

Peter walks to the home study

More than 98 per cent of the land will remain for agriculture and recreation.

center. It is located next to the living room. He seats himself in front of a small picture screen. Then he pushes the button marked *connect*. His home study unit is now hooked up to a central computer located 100 miles from his house.

"Hello, this is Peter," he types on the key board beneath the little screen. Peter watches as his message appears on the screen. After a moment his message disappears, and "Hello, Peter, what do you wish to do?" flashes in its place.

"Multiplication. Two-place numbers," Peter types.

An example appears on the screen in front of Peter:

$$72 \times 28$$

Peter sets up his work. He types:

$$\begin{array}{r} 28 \\ \underline{\times 72} \end{array}$$

"You are correct. Proceed to next step," flashes on the screen.

Peter types:

$$\begin{array}{r} 28 \\ \underline{\times 72} \\ 56 \\ \underline{193} \\ 1986 \end{array}$$

97

"Error" flashes on the screen. "Review multiplication tables 7 and 8."

Peter groans. He has been getting some of his multiplication facts mixed up lately. But he will practice them now. By tomorrow he should have them all under control.

Peter sits at the home study center for the next fifteen minutes, reviewing the two multiplication tables. When he is finished, he is able to do the original example correctly. A star flashes on the screen when Peter types "2016."

"You have done very well. What else do you wish to do?" appears on the screen.

"That is all for today. Thank you," Peter answers by typing the message on the keyboard.

Peter feels a little sleepy now. He goes to his room to take a nap. He is awakened after a while by a buzzing sound. It is his wireless phone letting him know that someone is calling him.

"TCA (telephone call accepted)," says Peter without getting up from his bed.

"Peter, it's Karl. How are you doing?"

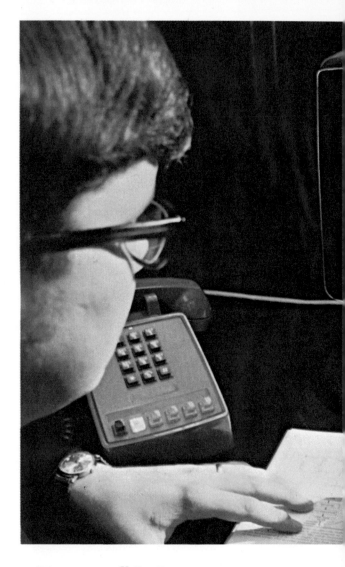

"Pretty well," Peter answers without getting up. "How was school today?"

"Oh, fine," Karl's voice says. "We had a ball game during lunch. You should have been there. We could have used you."

"I'll be back tomorrow," Peter says. "Thanks for calling. TCC."

A few minutes later, Peter gets up when he hears his parents come in. They're finally back. And they've got something with them. It's a pretty big box. About the size that could hold, say, a bicycle.

"Here it is," Mr. Smith says. "Model 6."

Peter is excited. And he is surprised to be getting his bicycle so early.

"Wow! Thanks!" he tells his parents. "But why did you go all the way to the merchandise center yourselves? You could have placed the order by phone and had the bicycle delivered."

Mrs. Smith explains. "In the old days," she says, "people actually used to go *out* of the house to shop for things. They went to places called stores. It was kind of exciting, we've heard. You could see and touch all the different things there were to choose from. Oh, sure. It had drawbacks. For one thing, it took longer than visionphone shopping. But we thought it would be fun to try it. So we drove to the merchandise center. We asked if we might be able to go in and pick out your bicycle ourselves. They looked at us as though we were crazy. But they let us in."

"Oh," says Peter, examining the gears on his new model 6. "How was it?"

"Great," says his mother. "It was really fun. Maybe some day soon we'll try it again."

We Could Be Friends

We could be friends
Like friends are supposed to be.
You, picking up the telephone
Calling me

    to come over and play
    or take a walk,
    finding a place
    to sit and talk,

Or just goof around
Like friends do,
Me, picking up the telephone
Calling you.

—Myra Cohn Livingston

What Do You Mean By That?

Did you hear about the children who wanted a snack? All they had was a calendar. So they ate dates.

That story is funny because *dates* has two different meanings. A *date* can mean "a particular day," such as May 9. A *date* can also mean "a type of fruit."

Many words have more than one meaning. When you read such a word, you need to know which meaning applies. You can usually tell by the way the word is used in the sentence. Read the following sentence:

I think what I'm doing is right.

The word *right* has more than one meaning. Sometimes, it means "correct." Other times, it means "the opposite of left." In the above sentence, the first meaning applies. You know because of the context clues in the sentence.

ACTIVITY A   Write each pair of sentences on your paper. Then read the two meanings for the underlined word. After each sentence, write the letter of the meaning that applies to the word in that sentence.

1. I am dressing now.
   The dressing tastes good.
   a. a sauce for salads
   b. putting on clothes

2. The rose is pink.
   He rose from the bed.
   a. a type of flower
   b. got up

3. Let's light a candle.
   This package is light.
   a. not heavy
   b. bright

4. A bat flew overhead.
   He swung the bat hard.
   a. an animal
   b. a wooden club

Read each sentence. Then read the meanings for the underlined word. On your paper, write the letter of the meaning that is used in the sentence.

1. We watched the men box for thirty minutes.
   a. a container   b. to fight with gloved fists

2. Duck behind the bushes so the raccoon won't see you.
   a. to bend down   b. a bird that swims

3. The lines of cars created a heavy traffic jam.
   a. a type of food   b. a crowded condition

4. Doctors train their assistants at the hospital.
   a. to teach   b. a line of railroad cars

5. I can fast for ten hours without getting hungry.
   a. quick, speedily   b. to go without food

6. The movie I saw last night was fair.
   a. a carnival   b. not very good, but not bad

7. We left the two-dollar bill as the waiter's tip.
   a. paper money   b. a list of money owed

8. Do you know how to run that machine?
   a. to move quickly   b. operate

9. Sheila broke the point of her pencil.
   a. a purpose   b. a sharp end

10. His sentence didn't have a subject or a predicate.
    a. time in prison   b. words stating an idea

11. She tied her hair in a bun.
    a. a hairstyle   b. a kind of roll or bread

12. She added another coat of paint.
    a. a layer   b. something to wear

13. He felt blue about missing the big game.
    a. in low spirits   b. a color

SIGNALS

Both human beings and animals communicate. Animals send and receive messages by using smell, touch, sight, and hearing. People do not have to rely solely on the senses to communicate. As human beings, we have a special ability to convey messages by using words. We are always looking for new and better ways to convey thoughts and feelings to others.

Thinking About "Signals"

1. How did the Associated Press improve communication among newspaper people?
2. What is the theme of "King Midas and the Golden Touch"? What does it say about money, people, and happiness?
3. How might you use language differently when (a) speaking to a baby, and (b) testifying before a committee of the U.S. Senate?
4. How does the written word make communication easier than using picture writing?
5. How can a television show like "Zoom" help children all over the country communicate?
6. In what ways do you communicate with and without words?
7. Think of something that has happened in your community or school that you are happy about or would like to see changed. Write a letter to the editor of your local newspaper to express your opinion.

Glossary

This glossary will help you to pronounce and to understand the meanings of some of the unusual or difficult words in this book.

The pronunciation of each word is printed beside the word in this way: **o·pen** (ō′pən). The letters, signs, and key words in the list below will help you read the pronunciation respelling. When an entry word has more than one syllable, a dark accent mark (′) is placed after the syllable that has the heaviest stress. In some words, a light accent mark (′) is placed after the syllable that receives a less heavy stress.

The pronunciation key, syllable breaks, accent mark placements, and phonetic respellings in this glossary are adapted from the Macmillan *School Dictionary* (1981) and the Macmillan *Dictionary* (1981). Other dictionaries may use other pronunciation symbols.

Pronunciation Key

a bad	**hw** white	**ô** off	**th** that	**ə** *stands for*
ā cake	**i** it	**oo** wood	**u** cup	a *as in* ago
ä father	**ī** ice	**ōo** food	**ur** turn	e *as in* taken
b bat	**j** joke	**oi** oil	**yōo** music	i *as in* pencil
ch chin	**k** kit	**ou** out	**v** very	o *as in* lemon
d dog	**l** lid	**p** pail	**w** wet	u *as in* helpful
e pet	**m** man	**r** ride	**y** yes	
ē me	**n** not	**s** sit	**z** zoo	
f five	**ng** sing	**sh** ship	**zh** treasure	
g game	**o** hot	**t** tall		
h hit	**ō** open	**th** thin		

A

ad · ver · tise (ad'vər tīz') *v.* **ad · ver · tised, ad · ver · tis · ing.** to make known to the public.

al · i · bi (al'ə bī') *n.* a claim or proof that one was somewhere else when a crime or other act was going on.

anx · ious (angk'shəs) *adj.* nervous, worried, or fearful about what may happen.

a · quar · i · um (ə kwer'ē əm) *n.* **1.** a tank, bowl, or other container in which fish, water animals, and plants are kept. **2.** a building that holds collections of fish, water animals, and water plants.

As · so · ci · at · ed Press (ə sō'shē āt'əd pres) a United States news agency that gathers and distributes news stories and pictures throughout the world.

Au · rum (ôr'əm)

au · to · mat · ic (ô'tə mat'ik) *adj.* **1.** acting, moving, or operating by itself. **2.** done without a person's control.

B

Bee · tho · ven, Lud · wig van (bā'tō'vən, lōōd'wig van) a German composer.

bo · nus (bō'nəs) *n.* something extra.

bribe (brīb) *n.* something offered or serving to influence or persuade. –*v.* to give or offer a bribe to.

C

ca · ble (kā'bəl) *n.* a bundle of wires that has a covering around it for protection. It is used to carry an electric current.

cap · tion (kap'shən) *n.* a title or written description for a picture.

car · ri · er pig · eon (kar'ē ər pij'ən) a homing pigeon.

Cat · a · lon (kat'ə lon)

cat · e · go · ry (kat'ə gôr'ē) *n.* a group or class of things.

ce · re · al (sēr'ē əl) *n.* a food that is made from grain. Oatmeal is a cereal.

chem · i · cal (kem'i kəl) *n.* a substance made by or used in chemistry.

clas · si · cal (klas' i kəl) *adj.* **1.** of or pertaining to the culture of ancient Greece and Rome. **2.** of the musical style that prevailed in Europe in the late part of the 18th century. **3.** of concert music or all music other than popular or folk music.

co · bra (kō'brə) *n.* a large, poisonous snake found in Africa and Asia. When a cobra becomes excited it spreads the skin about its neck so that it looks like a hood.

cobra

com · mer · cial (kə mur'shəl) *n.* an advertising message on radio or television.

com · mo · tion (kə mō'shən) *n.* a noisy confusion; disorder.

com · pete (kəm pēt') *v.* **com · pet · ed, com · pet · ing.** to strive against another or others, as in a contest.

con · ges · tion (kən jest'shən) *n.* **1.** an overcrowded or overburdened condition. **2.** a condition in which too much blood collects in an organ or tissue of the body.

Con · gres · sion · al Re · cord (kən gresh'ən əl rek'ərd) an account in writing of the proceedings of the United States Congress.

cov · er · age (kuv'ər ij) *n.* the reporting and publishing or broadcasting of news.

cym · bal (sim'bəl) *n.* a metal musical instrument that is shaped like a plate. One cymbal is hit against another to make a ringing sound.

D

date · line (dāt′līn′) *n.* a line in a piece of printed material that gives its date and place of origin.

death-de · fy · ing (deth′ di fī′ing) *adj.* challenging death.

de · cep · tive (di sep′ tiv) *adj.* misleading; meant to trick.

Dem · o · crat · ic (dem′ə krat′ik) *adj.* of or belonging to the Democratic Party, one of the two major political parties in the United States.

de · vice (di vīs′) *n.* something made or invented for a particular purpose.

dis · traught (di strôt′) *adj.* distracted; bewildered; deeply agitated.

dram · a · tize (dram′ə tīz′) *v.* **dram · a · tized, dram · a · tiz · ing.** **1.** to write or perform something as a play. **2.** to make something seem very exciting.

dredge (drej) *v.* **dredged, dredg · ing.** to clear out, deepen, or enlarge with a machine equipped for scooping up or removing mud, sand, and other substances from the bottom of a body of water.

E

ed · it (ed′it) *v.* to correct and check something so that it is ready to be printed.

e · di · tion (i dish′ən) *n.* one of a day's several printings of a newspaper.

ed · i · tor (ed′ə tər) *n.* a person who edits.

ed · i · to · ri · al (ed′ə tôr′ē əl) *n.* an article in a newspaper that expresses the opinions of the writer.

ef · fi · cient (i fish′ənt) *adj.* able to get the results wanted without wasting time and effort.

en · cour · age · ment (en kur′ij mənt) *n.* something that encourages or gives hope or confidence to.

er · ror (er′ər) *n.* something that is wrong; mistake.

ex · per · i · ment (eks per′ə mənt) *n.* a test that is used to discover or prove something.

ex · per · i · men · tal (eks per′ə ment′əl) *adj.* having to do with experiments.

ex · per · i · men · ter (eks per′ə ment′ər) *n.* one who experiments.

ex · plo · sion (eks plō′zhən) *n.* **1.** the act of bursting or expanding suddenly and noisily. **2.** a sudden outburst.

F

Fed · er · al Trade Com · mis · sion (fed′ər əl trād′ kə mish′ən) FTC; the government agency that protects consumers from misleading advertising.

fic · tion (fik′shən) *n.* a written work that tells a story about characters and events that are not real.

fi · na · le (fi na′lē) *n.* the last part of something; conclusion.

for · mu · la (fôr′myə lə) *n.* **1.** a set method of doing something. **2.** a set order of letters, symbols, or numbers that is used to express a rule or principle.

---

a **b**a**d**, ā **c**a**ke**, ä **f**a**ther**; e **p**e**t**, ē **me**; i **it**, ī **ice**; o **hot**, ō **open**, ô **off**; oo **wood**, ōō **food**; oi **oil**, ou **out**; th **thin**, <u>th</u> **that**; u **cup**, ur **turn**, yōō **music**; zh **treasure**; ə **ago**, tak**e**n, penc**i**l, lem**o**n, helpf**u**l

fra · grance (frā′grəns) *n.* a sweet or pleasing smell.

free · way frē′wā′) *n.* a highway with more than two lanes and no toll charges.

fu · ner · al (fyoo′nər əl) *n.* the ceremony for a dead person prior to burial or cremation.

G

gen · er · al pub · lic (jen′ər əl pub′lik) everyone; people in general.

gram (gram) *n.* a unit of weight in the metric system. One gram is equal to .035 ounces.

grasp (grasp) *v.* **1.** to take hold of firmly with the hand. **2.** to see the meaning of; understand.

grey · hound (grā′hound′) *n.* a slender dog with a smooth coat and a long nose. Greyhounds can run very fast.

H

hab · it (hab′it) *n.* an action that is done so often that it is done without thinking about it.

har · bor (här′bər) *n.* a sheltered place along a coast where ships and boats can anchor.

head · line (hed′līn′) *n.* one or more lines printed at the top of an article, as in a newspaper, that tells what the article is about.

hood (hood) *n.* **1.** a covering for the head and neck. **2.** something that looks like a hood or is used as a cover.

ho · ri · zon (hə rī′zən) *n.* the line where the sky and the ground or sea seem to meet.

house · lights (hous′lītz′) *n.* the lights in a theater that are used to illuminate the part of the theater where the audience sits.

I

il · lus · tra · tion (il′əs trā′shən) *n.* **1.** something used to make clear or explain. **2.** a picture or diagram.

i · mag · i · na · tion (i maj′ə nā′shən) *n.* the ability or power to create or form new images or ideas.

im · i · tate (im′ə tāt′) *v.* **im · i · ta · ted, im · i · ta · ting.** **1.** to try to act or behave like another person does; copy. **2.** to look like; resemble.

in · ter · na · tion · al (in′ tər nash′ə nəl) *adj.* having to do with or made up of two or more countries.

in · ves · ti · gate (in ves′ tə gāt′) *v.* **in · ves · ti · gat · ed, in · ves · ti · gat · ing.** to look into carefully in order to find facts and get information.

J

jump · line (jump′ līn′) *n.* a note in a newspaper telling a reader where an article is continued.

K

ki · lom · e · ter (ki lom′ə tər, kil′ə mē′tər) *n.* a unit of length in the metric system. A kilometer is equal to 1,000 meters, or about .62 of a mile.

L

la · ser (lā′zər) *n.* a device that produces an extremely powerful beam of light consisting of light waves that are of the same wavelength and are in phase.

Le · an · dra (lē an′drə)

lit · er (lē′tər) *n.* a basic unit of measurement in the metric system. A liter is equal to about 1.05 quarts of liquid.

lo · go (lō′gō) *n.* a symbol, letter, or word written in a particular way used as a trademark.

M

ma · jor (mā′jər) *adj.* bigger or more important.

meas · ure · ment (mezh′ər mənt) *n.* **1.** the size, height, or amount of something. **2.** a system of measuring.

mer · chan · dise (mur′chən dīz′, mur′chən dīs) *n.* things that are bought and sold.

me · ter (mē′tər) *n.* the basic unit of length in the metric system. A meter is equal to 39.37 inches, or slightly more than 3¼ feet.

met · ric (met′rik) *adj.* of or having to do with the metric system.

mi · cro · phone (mī′krə fōn′) *n.* a device that is used to transmit sound or to make it louder.

Mi · das (mī′dəs) *n.* a king in Greek legend who was given the power of turning everything he touched to gold.

min · i-sled (min′ē sled′) *n.* a skateboard with runners instead of wheels, used for sliding down snowcovered slopes.

mo · bile (mō′bēl) *n.* a piece of sculpture having delicately balanced units suspended in midair by wire or twine so that the individual parts can move independently, as when stirred by a breeze.

mol · ten (mōl′tən) *adj.* melted by heat.

N

near · sighted (nēr′sī′tid) *adj.* able to see objects that are close by more clearly than those that are far away.

net · work (net′wurk′) *n.* **1.** a system of lines or structures that cross. **2.** a group of radio or television stations that work together so that they can all broadcast the same program at the same time.

non · ver · bal (non vur′bəl) *adj.* not in words; not spoken.

No · va Sco · tia (nō′və skō′shə) a province of Canada, in the southeastern part of the country.

nu · tri · tion (noo trish′ən, nyoo trish′ən) *n.* food; nourishment.

O

ob · ser · va · tion (ob′zər vā′shən) *n.* **1.** the act or power of noticing. **2.** the fact of being seen; notice. **3.** something said; comment; remark.

o · pin · ion (ə pin′yən) *n.* a belief that is based on what a person thinks rather than on what is proved or known to be true.

o · ver · land (ō′vər land′) *adv.* **1.** by land. **2.** over or across the land.

P

par · tic · u · lar (pər tik′yə lər) *adj.* **1.** taken by itself; apart from others. **2.** having to do with some one person or thing. **3.** unusual in some way. **4.** very careful about details; hard to please.

---

a bad, ā cake, ä father; e pet, ē me; i it, ī ice; o hot, ō open, ô off; oo wood, o͞o food; oi oil, ou out; th thin, th that; u cup, ur turn, yo͞o music; zh treasure; ə ago, taken, pencil, lemon, helpful

per·mis·sion (pər mish'ən) *n.*   a con-
sent from someone in authority.

pi·geon (pij'ən) *n.*   a bird that has a
plump body, a small head, and thick,
soft feathers. Pigeons live in the wild
but are also found in nearly every city
of the world.

pint (pīnt) *n.*   a unit of measurement. It is
equal to half a quart.

pluck (pluk) *v.*   **1.** to pull off; pick. **2.** to pull
off hair or feathers from. **3.** to give a pull;
tug.

plunge (plunj) *v.*   **plunged, plung·ing.**
1. to put in forcefully. **2.** to dive or fall
suddenly.

por·poise (pôr'pəs) *n.*   an animal that is
warm-blooded and
lives in the ocean. A
porpoise has a round
head with a short,
blunt beak. Por-
poises are very intel-
ligent animals.

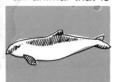

porpoise

por·tion (pôr'shən) *n.*   a part.

po·tion (pō'shən) *n.*   a drink, especially
one believed to have medicinal, magic, or
poisonous powers.

prac·ti·cal (prak'ti kəl) *adj.*   **1.** having to
do with real life; coming from experience.
2. sensible; down to earth.

pre·cau·tion (pri kô'shən) *n.*   something done beforehand to prevent harm or
danger.

pre·ci·sion (pri sizh'ən) *n.*   accuracy;
exactness.

pres·en·ta·tion   (prez'ən tā'shən,
prē'zən tā'shən) *n.*   the act of presenting
something.

proj·ect (proj'ekt') *n.*   a plan or activity to
be done.

pros·pec·tor (pros'pek tər) *n.*   a person
who explores for gold or other minerals.

pub·lish·er (pub'li shər) *n.*   a person or
company whose business is the produc-
ing and offering of printed material for sale
to the public.

Pu·litz·er Prize (pool'it sər prīz')   one of
a group of annual prizes in journalism, lit-
erature, music, and other fields, estab-
lished by Joseph Pulitzer.

quart (kwôrt) *n.*   a unit of measure. It is
equal to two pints.

ques·tion·naire (kwes'chə nār') *n.*   a
list of questions that is given to people to
answer. The answers are analyzed for
usable information.

R

ran·som (ran'səm) *n.*   **1.** the release of a
captive for a price. **2.** the price paid or
demanded before a captive is set free.
— *v.*   to get a captive set free by pay-
ing a price.

re·ac·tion (rē ak'shən) *n.*   an action in
response to something that has happened or has been done.

re·al·is·tic (rē'ə lis'tik) *adj.*   having to
do with what is real or practical.

re·al·i·ty   (rē al'ə tē)   *n. pl.,*
re·al·i·ties. an actual or true thing,
fact, or event.

re·hearse (ri hurs') *v.*   **re·hearsed,**
re·hears·ing. to practice or train in
order to prepare for a performance.

rep·re·sent·a·tive (rep'ri zen' tə tiv)
n. a person who is chosen to speak or act
for others. The members of the Congress
are our elected representatives in the
federal government.